Cesar Chavez

CESAR CHAVEZ

A PHOTOGRAPHIC ESSAY

Ilan Stavans

Cinco Puntos Press El Paso

FIRST EDITION
10 9 8 7 6 5 4 3 2 1

Library of Congress Cataloging-in-Publication Data

Stavans, Ilan.
 Cesar Chavez : a photographic essay / by Ilan Stavans. — 1st ed.
 p. cm.
 ISBN 978-1-933693-22-4 (alk. paper)
 1. Chavez, Cesar, 1927—Juvenile literature. 2. Migrant agricultural laborers—Labor unions—United States—Officials and employees—Biography—Juvenile literature. 3. Mexican Americans—Biography—Juvenile literature. I. Title.

 HD6509.C48S73 2010
 331.88'13092—dc22
 [B]

           2009044179

Front Cover: Cesar Chavez with unidentified older man
Image provided courtesy of the Cesar E. Chavez Foundation.

Back cover: Funeral procession for Cesar Chavez. Delano, California, 1993
Copyright © Ilka Hartmann 2010, www.ilkahartmann.com

Book design: JB Bryan / La Alameda Press

We draw our strength from despair.

Cesar Chavez
(1927-1993)

An Intimate Look
Ilan Stavans

Mention the name Cesar Chavez and you're likely to get a wide range of reactions, depending on the age of the person you ask. Is he a movie star? A senator? A boxer? Although most people recognize the name, they don't always connect it to his legacy. Few American icons get such a cold shoulder.

Why is this? The United States has long perceived itself through a black-and-white prism. Not many realize that during the Civil Rights Era, along with Reverend Martin Luther King's important protests against segregation, there were marches led by Cesar Chavez, Dolores Huerta, and other Chicano activists eager to improve the status of itinerant workers in Arizona, New Mexico, Colorado, Utah, Texas, California, and Oregon. Why is it that in chronicles of that period there is little mention of Mexicans, Puerto Ricans, and Filipinos who were fighting for their rights as well? The answer is that we approach race relations in this country almost exclusively through the legacy of slavery and emancipation. But we are that and much more: a true multiethnic tapestry. Yet other legacies remain suspiciously absent from our history books.

The silence doesn't occur just in history books. There are few museums and monuments commemorating this chapter of the 1960s. Monuments and buildings in Washington D.C. are devoted to the Holocaust, to the Middle Passage of Blacks from Africa to the United States, to the painful journey of American Indians since the arrival of the Mayflower in the seventeenth century. None is concerned with the plight of Spanish-speaking people, then and now. Why aren't the immigrants who risked their lives crossing the U.S.-Mexico border memorialized in our nation's capital?

Every generation looks at history with a fresh set of eyes. It finds what it looks for and discards what it considers of no value. The revitalization of grass-root activism by Barack Obama during his two-year presidential campaign and his election on November 4th, 2008, revived people's memories of the leaders of the '60s, but these were, for the most part, black leaders.

Chavez is a bridge to a more elastic understanding of the Civil Rights Era and, as such, a lens for viewing the nation's past in a broader, more comprehensive fashion. Rescuing him from the eclipse he is in is a step toward a wider, less exclusive understanding of who we are as a people. This is the appropriate time to embark on such task. The fight for change during the Civil Rights Era is now in full view. Immigration has reshaped the face of the United States. The average American is no longer white, of European ancestry. Newcomers from the so-called Third World—India, Pakistan, Korea, Vietnam, Central and Western Africa, the Caribbean, Mexico, Central and South America—are entering the middle class at a rapid pace.

Latinos, too, have changed. While Mexicans remain the largest component of Spanish speakers in the United States, other nationalities—Cubans, Dominicans, Nicaraguans, Guatemalans, and Colombians—have grown in number and influence. Chavez and his legacy used to represent Chicanos only, but that sort of compartmentalization is no longer possible. Chavez needs to be re-introduced to the young as a model in the larger fight against poverty and corporate abuse. It is crucial to reinstate him to the rightful place he deserves in United States history: as both a voice for and a champion of the oppressed.

As an immigrant from Mexico, I arrived to New York City in 1985. In Mexico, no one ever mentioned Chavez because the plight of Mexican Americans north of the border was a topic discussed only when one of our own relatives had embarked on the immigrant journey. Otherwise the real story of how Mexican people struggled day in and day out in the United States was seldom discussed.

I didn't hear much about Chavez in New York either. The majority of Latinos in the Northeast are from the Caribbean Basin. Their role in the Civil Rights Era was important, but Northeast and Southwest Latinos keep separate agendas. This is unfortunate because their immigrant experience is similar. And their heroes fight the same battles.

It was only when I stumbled upon a TV documentary and listened to Chavez deliver a speech on pesticides that I began to realize who he was. His eloquence hypnotized me. He was clearly angry but he controlled his emotions. His argument was both passionate and well-reasoned. He didn't use sophisticated words to impress his audience—Chavez was a common man speaking to people like himself.

In the following weeks, I looked for anything I could put my hands on that described his odyssey. Where did he come from? How did he become a civil rights leader? What kinds of experiences made him speak against the miserable life of migrant workers in California, Texas, New Mexico, Colorado, and Arizona? Was he raised speaking Spanish? What was his religious background?

The more I learned, the better I understood Chavez's motivations. He knew from personal experience what it meant to be poor, but he didn't let poverty shame him. He also understood that by explaining what oppression was like, he might convince the larger public that the situation of Mexican Americans and other laborers needed to change.

A child of immigrants, he dreamed of pursuing justice not just for a few but for all citizens. Chavez once said that "death comes to us all and we do not get to choose the time or the circumstance of our dying." And he added: "The hardest thing of all is to die rightly."

This is not to say that he is a leader beyond reproach. His later years were marked by the disintegration of the labor union achievements he had accomplished throughout his life. Needless to say, the change was not exclusively his: the nation as a whole had undergone dramatic changes. In the 1980s, the overall mood was less about activism than about consent and careerism. In spite of these things, he remains a fascinating leader, human in his defects, titanic in his aspirations.

Several years ago, I traveled to Detroit to the Farm Workers Archive at the Walter P. Reuther Library, College of Urban, Labor and Metropolitan Affairs, Wayne State University, to research his speeches and correspondence. My research culminated in a collection I edited called *An Organizer's Tale*. To my surprise, I also came across a treasure trove of images, taken primarily by amateurs, which spans almost seven decades. Taken together, these images offer an intimate, humane glimpse of Chavez the man through the eyes of those who knew him best.

To the Reuther photos, I've added an array of snapshots found at the Cesar E. Chavez Foundation, the majority of which were taken by amateur photographers. These iconic images were made available to me through the generosity of Paul E. Parks, Esq. I've completed the overall portrait with material from news organizations, academic institutions, and independent photographers. Collecting the material has posed a number of challenges, including identifying the date and place of the photograph as well as the person responsible for the snapshot. Whenever possible, I've listed this information. I've organized the photographs using a semblance of chronology, although I've broken the sequence wherever the narrative required visual consistency. To enliven the material, I've provided historical, biographical, and philosophical context, at times quoting Chavez directly. Since this context is impressionistic in nature, I've included a thorough chronology at the end of the volume.

Cesar Chavez lives in the memory of an older generation and now in the hands of a younger one.

A Photographic Essay

Cesar Chavez, six years old, with his sister

Born on a small farm near Yuma, Arizona, Cesar Chavez entered the whirlpool of itinerant labor as a child after his family lost possession of their ranch. They moved wherever the harvest took them. He was part of a generation of Mexican Americans—the term "Chicano," in circulation since the 1920s, became fashionable in the '60s—whose heritage lay in Mexico. Once they crossed the border, though, they became an integral part of the fabric of the United States. Cesar spoke unschooled Spanish, but, as he later recalled, teachers insisted migrant children learn English. "They said that if we were American," he recalled, "then we should speak the language, and if we wanted to speak Spanish, we should go back to Mexico."

"All my life, I have been driven by one dream, one goal, one vision: To overthrow a farm labor system in this nation which treats farm workers as if they were not important human beings. Farm workers are not agricultural implements. They are not beasts of burden—to be used and discarded. That dream was born in my youth. It was nurtured in my early days of organizing. It has flourished. It has been attacked.

"I'm not very different from anyone else who has ever tried to accomplish something with his life. My motivation comes from my personal life—from watching what my mother and father went through when I was growing up; from what we experienced as migrant farm workers in California. That dream, that vision, grew from my own experience with racism, with hope, with the desire to be treated fairly and to see my people treated as human beings and not as chattel. It grew from anger and rage—emotions I felt 40 years ago when people of my color were denied the right to see a movie or eat at a restuarant in many parts of California. It grew from the frustration and humiliation I felt as a boy who couldn't understand how the growers could abuse and exploit farm workers when there were so many of us and so few of them.

"Later, in the '50s, I experienced a different kind of exploitation. In San Jose, in Los Angeles and in other urban communities, we—the Mexican American people—were dominated by a majority that was Anglo. I began to realize what other minority people had discovered: That the only answer—the only hope—was in organizing. More of us had to become citizens. We had to register to vote. And people like me had to develop the skills it would take to organize, to educate, to help empower the Chicano people.

"[. . .] Deep in my heart, I knew I could never be happy unless I tried organizing the farm workers. I didn't know if I would succeed. But I had to try. All Hispanics—urban and rural, young and old—are connected to the farm workers' experience. We had all lived through the fields—or our parents had. We shared that common humiliation. How could we progress as a people, even if we lived in the cities, while the farm workers—men and women of our color—were condemned to a life without pride? How could we progress as a people while the farm workers—who symbolized our history in this land—were denied self-respect? How could our people believe that their children could become lawyers and doctors and judges and business people while this shame, this injustice was permitted to continue?"

—*Cesar Chavez*
November 9, 1984

Eighth-grade graduation picture, 1942. Chavez quit school after this to work full time in the fields.

Chavez in the U.S. Navy, 1947.

Chavez's schooling was constantly interrupted. He later on recalled that he attended some thirty elementary and middle schools. The experience left him scarred. In an interview, Chavez recalled that getting to school was a chore. "I never liked it. They made me go, so I went, but they always had to push me to go. It wasn't the learning I hated, but the conflicts. The teachers were very mean. I also didn't like sitting in the classroom. I was bored to death. I'd just go to sleep. Once the teacher even sent me a note home saying I was ill, that I had to be taken to a doctor because I was always falling asleep."

After the eighth grade, he quit school and worked in the fields to help support the family. World War II was under way and Chavez, like thousands of other *mexicanos*, was ready to serve his country. He wanted to flee from the harsh working conditions that beat him down day after day—heat, exhaustion, boredom, and low pay—and joined the Navy as a deck hand.

Chavez joined the Navy when he was seventeen. He would later on describe that time as "the two worst years of my life." He didn't yet have a sense of direction for his life. And he encountered strong anti-Mexican feelings in other cadets.

Shortly before he joined the Navy, his family had moved to Delano, California. When his military service was finished, he returned to Delano and married his highschool sweetheart, Helen Fabela.

Helen and Cesar Chavez with their children, circa 1968. The couple had eight children,
six of them pictured here: (bottom row, from left to right) Fernando, Linda, Paul;
(top row, from left to right) Eloise, Sylvia, and Anthony

The Chavez family moved to San José and lived in a neighboorhood nicknamed *Sal Si*
Puedes ("Escape if you can"), where they joined the congregation of Father Donald McDonnell.
It was through Father McDonnell that Chavez began to read voraciously and became
mesmerized by St. Francis, who preached absolute humility. Mahatma Gandhi's philosophy of
nonviolence also captured Chavez's imagination.

Braceros boarding a bus to go to California agricultural fields, 1958.
Chavez was just beginning his career as an organizer.

Braceros riding a farm truck, 1950s.

Artwork used on the cover of the United Farm Workers publication Pesticides: The Poisons We Eat, *1967.*

Life for migrant workers meant no home, no secure job, not even the promise of food after a day in the fields. It was a nerve-wracking existence. Families felt uprooted; the Chavezes, and hundreds of others like them, didn't belong anywhere. Chavez looked back on his early years as a period of anxiety and was appalled by how widespread the sense of deprivation was. In "An Organizer's Tale," a piece he wrote about his ordeal, he stated: "There are vivid memories from my childhood—what we had to go through because of low wages and the conditions, basically because there was no union." Conscious of the poor conditions of labor workers, he began contemplating a way to help. His thoughts moved in the direction of a union that would bring workers' needs to the attention of the owners and, if they failed to act, to the government authorities.

Chavez's attitude was that the best way to solve problems was in a peaceful manner. "Many people feel that an organization that uses nonviolent methods to reach its objectives must continue winning victories one after another in order to remain nonviolent," he said once. "If that be the case, then a lot of efforts have been miserable failures. There is a great deal more involved than victories. My experience has been that the poor know violence more intimately than most people because it has been a part of their lives, whether the violence of the gun or the violence of want and need."

Chavez added: "I don't subscribe to the belief that nonviolence is cowardice, as some militant groups are saying. In some instances, nonviolence requires more militancy than violence. Nonviolence forces you to abandon the shortcut in trying to make a change in the social order. Violence, the shortcut, is the trap people fall into when they begin to feel that it is the only way to attain their goal. When these people turn to violence, it is a very savage kind."

Chavez identified with Mexican revolutionary figure Emiliano Zapata.

Fred Ross Jr., the director of the Community Service Organization, c. 1970s.

Chavez met Fred Ross, the founder of the Community Service Organization. It was an important meeting. Ross was an outsider who gave himself to the work of improving labor conditions. He was very much aware of the substantial number of Mexican Americans working in the fields in California, Texas, Colorado, and Arizona. He was looking to recruit an insider who was able to speak Spanish and to communicate with Mexican-American workers on their own terms.

Community Service Organization with Chavez second from lower right, c. 1950s.

Chavez, Fred Ross, Luis Valdez and Dolores Huerta at an unidentified meeting, c. late 1980s

The friendship between the two lasted until Ross' death two decades later. At Ross' funeral in San Francisco on October 17, 1992, Chavez offered a eulogy in which he chronicled their lasting relationship: "Fred used to say, 'You can't take shortcuts, because you'll pay for it later.' He believed society would be transformed from within by mobilizing individuals and communities. But you have to convert one person at a time, time after time. Progress only comes when people just plow ahead and do it. It takes lots of patience. The concept is so simple that most people miss it."

Ross enlisted Chavez. Between 1952 and 1962, the two organized twenty-two CSO chapters across California. With the help of Chavez's leadership, CSO became the most effective Latino civil rights group of its day. It helped Latinos become citizens and gain the right to vote.

Chavez, lower right, organizing for the Community Service Organization, c. 1950s.

The 1960s were formative for Chavez. By 1962, at the age of thirty-five, he had learned his lesson—he realized that migrant workers were a largely underrepresented class and that nobody in the power circles, whether in California or Washington, gave a damn about them. Workers needed a leader with an authentic style, ready to air their claims. Furthermore, he understood that, with the proper orchestration, the power of the people was enormous. What they needed to do was to join forces, to work in unity.

Chavez's strategy was to first establish a farm worker's organization, and then to arrange a national convention in which its mission would be established. Indeed, on September 20, 1962, such a gathering of the National Farm Workers Association (NFWA) convened in Fresno, California, in an abandoned theater. By underlining the national, not the regional, Chavez sought to build a structure with far-reaching influence. About one hundred and fifty delegates and their families attended the convention. Members voted to organize the farm workers and elect temporary officers. They agreed to lobby for a minimum wage law covering farm workers. The term *la causa*, the cause, was embraced. The motto of the convention was "¡Viva La Causa!"

At a speech he delivered at Harvard in March 1970, Chavez said: "Organizing farm workers is very different from organizing any other workers in the country today. Here we don't have any rules, any regulations. We don't have any prescribed methods, no precedents. There is no law for farm labor organizing, save the law of the jungle. The citizens and their rights for seven years have been ignored and the employers have seen to it that they don't survive."

Chavez, c. 1960s.

Farmworkers gathering melons in California.

The dire conditions, including long working hours, undrinkable water, unhealthy living quarters, and a meager diet, prompted the Union to seek change through political means.

Farmworkers harvesting onions, c. 1970s.

*Workers using the short-handled hoe, a tool that came to symbolize the exploitation
that farm workers were subjected to for decades in California.*

The concept of *la huelga*, the strike, is an integral part of labor history. During the Industrial Revolution, it was strictly prohibited. The rise of social democracy as a philosophy of labor relations at the end of the nineteenth century and the beginning of the twentieth established it as a right of workers.

Chavez studied a number of strikes, including the one in Cananea, in the Mexican state of Sonora, in 1906, against the Cananea Consolidated Copper Company owned by the U.S. colonel William C. Greene. As portrayed by historians, the copper company made the decades-long dictatorship of Porfirio Díaz all the more unpopular and triggered the Mexican Revolution four years later.

By organizing migrant workers, Chavez took *la huelga* to unforeseen heights. He scheduled marches, which, at a time when the American news media was consolidating its status as an independent tool in the democratic dialogue, became spectacular events.

Chavez, 1965.

The Delano Strike was to become the first stepping stone for the farmworkers and their union. It was a dangerous struggle and lasted five years. As a leader, Chavez had identified a genuine feeling of solidarity among his constituents. "The people who took part in the strike and the march have something more than their material interest going for them," he said later on. "If it were only material, they wouldn't have stayed on the strike long enough to win. It is difficult to explain. But it flows out in the ordinary things they say. For instance, some of the younger guys are saying, 'Where do you think it's going to be, the next strike?'

"I say, 'Well, we have to win in Delano.'

"They say, 'We'll win, but where do we go next?'

"I say, 'Maybe most of us will be working in the fields.'

"They say, 'No, I don't want to go and work in the fields. I want to organize. There are a lot of people that need our help.'

"So I say, 'You're going to be pretty poor then, because when you strike you don't have much money.'

"They say they don't care much about that. It is bigger, certainly, than just a strike."

The tools used by the movement to achieve its goals had at their core a nonviolent ideology. Resistance was seen through pacifist eyes. Employing boycotts, strikes, and other forms of community organizing, the movement gained national attention. The apex of the fight came in 1970, when the United Farm Workers union bargained a contract with the table-grape owners that brought better conditions to over thousands of workers.

A family picket line.

Striker trying to rally workers. "We are suffering," Chavez said.
"We have suffered. And we aren't afraid to suffer to win our cause."

Picketers in the Coachella Valley of California, 1968.

United Farm Workers Union Flag.

Chavez's pursuit became part of *El Movimiento*, as the Chicano Movement came to be known. Other Mexican Americans became active, under the leadership of figures like Reies López Tijerina and Rodolfo "Corky" González.

His intention was to alter, once and for all, the marginalized status of Mexican Americans in the United States and to put an end to segregation practices which, over time, resulted in an alienated mentality. The movement included intellectuals (Luis Valdez), newsmen and radio broadcasters (Rubén Salazar), muralists (Yolanda López, Rupert García), as well as students, teachers, and housewives.

Luis Valdez's theater troupe *El Teatro Campesino*, made up of farm laborers, staged short plays called *actos* at rallies to promote political awareness, and shifted to *mitos*, pieces about symbols in Mexican history, thus assisting Chavez. The concept of *La Raza*, the race, served as glue. It was intimately linked to *mestizaje*, the process of miscegenation whereby the European colonizers in the New World mixed with the aboriginal population.

Chavez often went out of his way to distinguish between *El Movimiento* and *La Causa*. He wasn't a symbol for all Chicanos, he declared. His central drive was to better workers' lives; it was not the radical makeover of an entire ethnic minority. Of course, insofar as his cause helped advance change for Mexican Americans, he was delighted. What was essential, in his view, was that change took place sooner rather than later. He affirmed: "We want to be recognized, yes, but not with a glowing epitaph on our tombstone."

Luis Valdez (center) performing with El Teatro Campesino, 1966.

Paul Chavez, Cesar's son, with United Farm Workers attorney Marcos Camacho.

Chavez addressing a rally, c. 1970s.

*José Martinez, Dolores Huerta, Tony Orendain, and Chavez at the founding
of the National Farmworkers Association, Fresno, California, 1962*

Among the people Chavez collaborated with was Dolores Huerta. A co-founder of the
National Farm Workers Association, Huerta lived under Chavez's shadow for decades. Yet
Huerta led the grape boycott and negotiated various contracts for the farm workers, including
the one in 1970 in which the California grape industry signed a three-year contract.

Throughout her life, she has actively fought for the improvement of conditions for Mexicans.
She campaigned in favor of putting driver's license examinations in California in Spanish, for
the 1973 Agricultural Labor Relations Act, and for abortion rights. Her views have at times put
her at odds with the conservative wing of the Latino community.

Huerta and other feminists have frequently argued that the Chicano Movement has been,
at its core, a macho enterprise. Although women were enlisted in the cause, they were—not
surprisingly—relegated to a second rank.

Dolores Huerta speaks with grape harvesters in a field during a break from work, 1969.

Dolores Huerta leads supporters of the UFW in an unidentified march.

Dolores Huerta and Chavez meet with farmworkers and supporters.

Dolores Huerta speaking at a meeting.

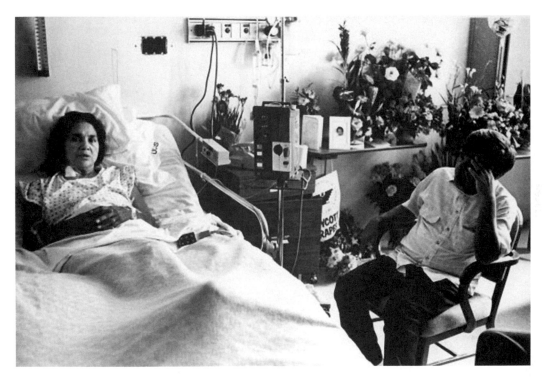

Chavez visits with Dolores Huerta as she recuperates in the hospital after being assaulted by the police. The assault occurred during a protest rally against President George H.W. Bush in San Francisco, California in 1988. Huerta was beaten with a police baton, resulting in several broken ribs and a destroyed spleen.

Chavez at a rally of the United Automobile Workers, 1974.

Chavez's efforts were not exclusively about Mexican Americans and Filipinos. He once wrote: "When people are involved in something constructive, trying to bring about change, they tend to be less violent than those who are not engaged in rebuilding or in anything creative. Nonviolence forces one to be creative; it forces any leader to go to the people and get them involved so that they can come forth with new ideas. I think that once people understand the strength of nonviolence—the force it generates, the love it creates, the response that it brings from the total community—they will not be willing to abandon it easily." Chavez represented Puerto Ricans, Blacks, and other underserved minorities. He organized them to resist, in nonviolent ways, the oppressive labor conditions they were subjected to and to have a collective bargaining voice. Nonviolence was his trademark.

Chavez being interviewed by Radio Campesina.

Jerry Cohen, Chavez and LeRoy Chatfield outside the Kern County courthouse, Bakersfield, California, after attending a contempt hearing, February, 1968. Chavez had been fasting to protest the treatment of farm workers during the Delano Strike. This was the thirteenth day of his fast.

Paul Chavez (son of Cesar Chavez), Chávez, and Jerry Cohen. Salinas, 1975.

Chavez's worldview was defined by his devout Catholic faith. "God writes in exceedingly crooked lines," Chavez wrote. As a nation, Mexico has a *mestizo* identity shaped by a religious sentiment brought along by the Spanish conquistadors. He identified with Christ's teachings. "I've read what Christ said," he said once. "He was very clear in what he meant and knew exactly what he was after. He was extremely radical, and he was for social change."

But Chavez was weary of the Catholic Church as an institution. "It's common knowledge," he wrote, "that the Catholic Church is a block of power in society and that the property and purchase of the Church rate second only to the government." He challenged bishops, priests, and the clergy in general to take action. "To build power among Mexican Americans presents a threat to the Church; to demand reform of Anglo-controlled institutions stirs up dissension... However, if representatives of the Church are immobilized and compromised into silence, the Church will not only remain irrelevant to the real needs and efforts of La Raza in the barrios; but our young leaders of today will continue to scorn the Church and view it as an obstacle to their struggle for social, political and economic independence."

Chavez went on a European tour in 1974 to spread his gospel. In quick succession, he visited England, Norway, Italy, Switzerland, Denmark, Belgium, and France, among other places. In Rome he had a twenty-minute audience with Pope Paul VI. "To see the Pope is a big thing in Europe," he wrote in his rough-and-tumble travelogue, "not just religiously but politically."

Chavez meets with Pope Paul VI, Rome, Italy, 1974.

Meeting between Rabbi Guthman and Chavez during Yom Kippur, 1971.

Chavez speaks during the funeral mass for Juan de la Cruz, Arvin, California, August, 1973. Juan de la Cruz was shot and killed while walking on a United Farm Workers picket line.

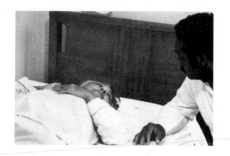

Rev. Jesse Jackson visits Chavez during a fast, 1988.

Perhaps the single most provocative facet of Chavez's career was his self-immolation. He used religious imagery (the term *pilgrimage*, to begin with) to emphasize his message. The centerpieces of that message were the concepts of suffering and sacrifice. "We're suffering," he contended. "And we're not afraid to suffer more in order to win our cause." And: "It takes a lot of punishment to achieve change…"

His supreme sacrifice came in the form of a series of fasts he embarked on over a period of almost two decades. In February of 1968, after several discouraged strikers began to contemplate the use of violence against growers, he fasted to encourage his members to adhere to nonviolence. The response was overwhelming: 8,000 farm workers, as well as California Senator Robert F. Kennedy, attended a mass to break Chavez's 25-day fast. Clearly, by now he had become an emblem.

In a famous scene filled with religious meaning, Kennedy gave Chavez a piece of bread and called him "one of the heroic figures of our time." Only six days after the fast ended, Bobby Kennedy announced his candidacy for the presidency. Not long after that, he was assassinated.

Chavez's fasts were entwined with his understanding of Christ's legacy. He lived to say it openly: "When any person suffers for someone in greater need, that person is human." In his view, the poor had a "tremendous capacity to suffer." It was a matter of suffering with some kind of hope, rather than with no hope at all. Clearly he had internalized the pathos of his constituency, establishing a bridge between his own physical being and the farm-working community at large. The agony of one was the distress of the other. He recognized his own value by suffering in public, which isn't an element of the Hispanic character, more prone to experiencing pain in private.

Robert Kennedy and Chavez the day Chavez broke his 25-day fast, 1968.

Chavez the day he broke his fast, 1968.

Chavez remains unrecognized as he joins an anti-Chavez demonstration in Hartford, Connecticut, 1969.

Chavez walks to the Monterey County Jail, surrounded by supporters, Salinas, California, 1970.
Chavez was jailed for 20 days for refusing to obey a court order to stop the boycott against Bud Antle lettuce.

Funeral procession, August 1973. Over 7,000 mourners march with the casket of the slain farm worker Nagi Daifullah en route to his funeral at Forty Acres, Delano, California. Daifullah was a 24-year-old picket captain of Yemeni descent who died after being struck in the skull by a police flashlight. Chavez stands to the left of the American flag, Dolores Huerta stands to the right.

The union and the strike were two of Chavez's devices, to which he soon added a third: the boycott. He started a grape boycott. Members followed grape trucks and set up picket lines wherever grapes were sold in the country. The growers were distraught and bitterly complained of bias against them. Oftentimes, they brought in *braceros* to substitute for the striking field workers or to cut deals with immigration officials to hire illegal workers without risk of penalties or worker deportation.

The grape boycott put Chavez in the international spotlight during the 1970s. Grape strikers spread across North America in an effort to start an international grape boycott. The nation tuned in. Supporters outside supermarkets and grocery stores from New York to Illinois, from Ohio to Arizona, displayed their embrace of Chavez and the marchers. That spring and summer, most California table-grape growers signed contracts with the United Farm Workers. Chavez then called for a national boycott of lettuce.

Chavez speaking during the boycott, c. 1973.

Boycott pickets at a produce terminal, c. 1971.

Pickets supporting the Gallo boycott, c. 1971.

Grape boycott pickets, 1970s.

Signing a boycott petition on a New York City subway.

Procession of mourners enroute to the funeral of Rufino Contreras, 1979.

El Movimiento had dozens of martyrs. One of them was Mexican-American striker Rufino Contreras, who was shot dead in an Imperial Valley lettuce field by a foreman on February 10, 1979. Four days later at his funeral, Chavez turned Contreras into a martyr for *El Movimiento*. "The day of Contreras' death," Chavez said, was a day that should live in infamy, "a day without joy. The sun didn't shine. The birds didn't sing. The rain didn't fall."

He went on to say: "What is the worth of a man? What is the worth of a farm worker? Rufino, his father and brother together gave the company twenty years of their labor. They were faithful workers who helped build up the wealth of their boss, helped build up the wealth of his ranch. What was their reward for their service and their sacrifice? When they petitioned for a more just share of what they themselves produced, when they spoke out against the injustice they endured, the company answered them with bullets; the company sent hired guns to quiet Rufino Contreras."

Pickets outside a vineyard.

Chavez talking to farmworkers, late 1970s

Chavez addressing a rally, 1990s.

During the vigil, streams of people arrived all night until the early morning hours—
some from as far away as Arizona—to pay their respects to Chavez. Delano, California, April 31, 1993.

Cesar Chavez died on April 23, 1993. A few days after his death, 40,000 mourners marched behind his pine casket in Delano. Peter Matthiessen, then working as a journalist for *The New Yorker* and a man who knew Chavez well, wrote an obituary. "With the former scourge of California safely in his coffin," Matthiessen said, "state flags were lowered to half-mast by order of the Governor and messages poured forth from the heads of Church and State, including the Pope and the President of the United States. This last of the marches was enormous."

"We have lost perhaps the greatest Californian of the twentieth century," the president of the California State Senate said, in public demotion of Cesar Chavez's sworn enemies Nixon and Reagan.

Matthiessen added that "anger was a part of Chavez, but so was a transparent love of humankind. The gentle mystic that his disciples wished to see inhabited the same small body as the relentless labor leader who concerned himself with the most minute operation of his union. Astonishingly—this seems to me his genius—the two Cesars were so complementary that without either, La Causa could not have survived."

Relatives and friends carrying the coffin of Chavez, 1993.

How does one die the right death? By making one's life meaningful to others. By leaving an imprint. By opening a road for others to follow. Chavez's message will die with him unless we follow his lead in making America more open, a country with economic equality for all, where the color of one's skin is not an expression of one's character. He wanted to live in a country which was truly democratic, where tolerance and dignity are available to all. "We are working toward creating the new man," he said once, "the man who will think of the common good, as you and I do, instead of the man who thinks of himself first."

President William Jefferson (Bill) Clinton posthumously presents the Presidential Medal of Freedom for Chavez to Helen Chavez, White House, Washington, DC, August 8, 1994.

Chronology

March 31, 1927: Cesario Estrada Chavez is born on a small farm near Yuma, Arizona, to Librado and Juana Chavez.

August 29, 1937: The state takes possession of Librado Chavez's ranch.

1938: Librado Chavez leaves home in August with several relatives to look for work in California. He soon finds a job threshing beans in Oxnard, a small town near the coast about fifty-five miles north of Los Angeles. Librado writes home to Juana telling her to come with the children. The Chavezes become a family of migrant workers.

1941: Chavez has his first contact with a union when a Congress of Industrial Organizations (CIO) member comes to the Chavez house to talk to Librado and his brother about organizing with other workers.

1942: Chavez quits school after the eighth grade. He begins full-time work in the fields to help his father support the family.

1944: At the age of seventeen, Chavez is tired from the physical strain of sugar beet thinning. He joins the Navy to get away from farm labor and works as a deck hand, a job assigned to most Mexican Americans in the Navy. While visiting his home in Delano on a seventy-two-hour leave, Chavez and his friends go to a local theater. Chavez is arrested after refusing to give up his seat in the left-hand section reserved for Anglo and Japanese customers.

1948: Chavez marries Helen Fabela with whom he eventually has eight children. In the late forties, Chavez and his family join the congregation of Father Donald McDonnell in their San Jose barrio *Sal Si Puedes*. Father McDonnell introduces Chavez to the writings of the Encyclicals,

St. Francis, and Gandhi as well as to the transcripts of the Senate LaFollette Committee hearings which were held in Los Angeles in 1940.

1952: In June, while Chavez is working in an apricot orchard outside San Jose, Fred Ross, founder of the Community Service Organization (CSO), recruits him to become an active member of CSO.

1952-1962: Chavez and Fred Ross organize twenty-two CSO chapters across California. With the help of Chavez's leadership, CSO is the most effective Latino civil rights group of its day. Chavez and his organizers helped Latinos become citizens and gain the right to vote.

March 31, 1962: Chavez resigns from the CSO to dedicate himself fulltime to organizing farm workers. He and his family move to Delano so that he can start building the foundations of his organization.

September 30, 1962: The first convention of Chavez's National Farm Workers Association (NFWA) convenes in an abandoned theater in Fresno. About one hundred and fifty delegates and their families attend the convention. Members vote to organize the farm workers, elect temporary officers, agree to lobby for a minimum wage law covering farm workers and adopt "*¡Viva La Causa!*" as a motto.

1962-1965: Chavez works continously to build up the membership of his union. In spring 1965, the NFWA organizes its first strike against the rose growers. On September 16, 1965, the association joins a strike against the grape growers in the Delano area. One thousand two hundred workers join the strike on the first day. The Delano Grape Strike lasts five years. NFWA begins a grape boycott in the months of November and December. Members follow grape trucks and set up picket lines wherever grapes are sold.

1966: To draw interest in the farm workers' cause, Chavez and strikers from the NFWA and Agricultural Workers Organizing Committee (AWOC) embark on a 340-mile pilgrimage from Delano to the steps of the Capitol in Sacramento in March and April. Organizers of the NFWA devise *El Plan de Delano* (The Plan of Delano) to outline the rights of farm workers. During the march, and four months into the grape boycott, Schenley Vineyards signs a contract with the NFWA. It's the first contract between a grower and a farm workers' union in United States history. The NFWA calls a strike and a boycott against DiGiorgio Fruit Corporation that lasts from the spring to the summer. The union forces the grower to hold an election among its workers. In response, the company brings in the Teamsters to oppose Chavez's NFWA. The NFWA and AWOC decide to merge and create the United Farm Workers Association (UFWA) and DiGiorgio workers vote for the UFWA. During the DiGiorgio struggle, Martin Luther King, Jr. sends a telegram to Chavez offering fellowship and good will. In his letter, Dr. King wishes Chavez and his members continuing success in their fight for equality.

1967: The UFWA goes after Giumarra, the largest table-grape grower. Nearly all of Giumarra's workers join in the strike, but many workers return to the field days later. The UFWA then imposes a boycott of Giumarra products, but when the boycott begins to become effective, Giumarra changes its labeling. The UFWA decides to boycott all California table grapes.

1968: In February, after several discouraged strikers contemplate the use of violence against growers, Chavez embarks on his first fast to encourage his members to adhere to nonviolence. Eight thousand farm workers as well as Senator Robert F. Kennedy attend a mass to break Chavez's 25-day fast. Kennedy gives Chavez a piece of bread and calls him "one of the heroic figures of our time." Six days after the fast ends, Robert Kennedy announces his candidacy for the presidency of the United States.

1967-1970: The grape boycott is in the international spotlight. Grape strikers spread across North America in an effort to impose an international grape boycott.

1970: Most California table-grape growers sign UFWA contracts in the spring and summer. Chavez calls for a national boycott of lettuce after Salinas Valley growers sign contracts with the Teamsters Union to help keep the UFWA out of the fields. On December 10, the UFWA singles out Bud Antle on the lettuce boycott. Chavez is arrested and jailed for ignoring the injunction prohibiting the UFWA from boycotting Antle. Coretta Scott King, widow of the Reverend Martin Luther King, Jr., and Ethel Kennedy, widow of Robert Kennedy, pay Chavez a visit in jail.

1971: UFWA membership grows to eighty thousand. Headquarters for the union move to La Paz, in Keene, California.

1972: The UFWA becomes an independent affiliate of the AFL-CIO. The United Farm Workers Association becomes the United Farm Workers of America. To avoid a possible attack by the UFWA, the American Farm Bureau Federation, along with other grower organizations and extreme right-wing groups, start legislation in California and other states outlawing boycotts and strikes at harvest time, and setting up election procedures geared to allow only a few people to decide whether a union will be welcome. Bills are passed in Kansas, Idaho, and Arizona. Between May 11 and June 4, Chavez fasts in Phoenix to protest the recent legislation.

1973: Rather than renew their three-year contract with the UFWA, table-grape growers sign contracts in the spring and summer with the Teamsters without an election. In the Coachella and San Joaquin valleys, thousands of grape workers begin a three-month strike. Strikers are arrested, beaten, and shot for violating anti-picketing injunctions. To prevent further violence, Chavez calls off the strike and begins a second grape boycott.

1973-1975: A Louis Harris poll shows that millions of Americans are boycotting grapes, Gallo wine, and lettuce. Approximately seventeen million Americans are boycotting grapes. In June 1975, growers agree to a state law guaranteeing California farm workers the right to organize and bargain with their employers. Chavez gets the Agricultural Labor Relations Act through the state legislation once Jerry Brown becomes governor. In the mid-to-late 70s, the UFWA wins the majority of the elections it participates in. It signs contracts with a large number of growers. The Teamsters Union signs a "jurisdictional" agreement with the UFWA, agreeing to leave the fields.

1978: The UFWA calls off its boycotts of grapes, Gallo wine, and lettuce.

1979: From January to October, the UFWA continues to strike growers to negotiate better wages and benefits. Striker Rufino Contreras is shot dead in a lettuce field by a foreman. Chavez delivers Contreras' eulogy. In the early '80s, with the aid of one million dollars in growers' contributions, George Deukmejian is elected governor of California.

1983-1990: Governor Deukmejian stops enforcing California's farm labor law. As a result, thousands of farm workers lose their UFWA contracts and their jobs. In 1983, worker René López is shot after voting in a Union election. In 1984, Chavez declares a third grape boycott. To make the public aware of how pesticides were poisoning grape workers and their children, he launches the "Wrath of Grapes" campaign. Between July and August 1988, Chavez, at the age of sixty-one, embarks on his last and longest fast, which lasted thirty-six days. In the early '90s, he continues the third grape boycott.

1992: Chavez and the UFWA's Vice President, Arturo Rodriguez, lead vineyard walkouts from the spring to the summer in the Coachella and San Joaquin valleys. With the help of the walkout, grape workers win their first industry-wide pay hike in eight years.

April 23, 1993: Chavez dies in his sleep. On April 29, 1993, 40,000 mourners march behind Chavez's pine casket in Delano.

1994: On the anniversary of Chavez's passing, UFWA president Arturo Rodriguez leads a march retracing Chavez's pilgrimage from Delano to Sacramento. Seventeen thousand farm workers join together on the steps of the state Capitol to kick off another UFWA contract-negotiating campaign. On August 8, President Bill Clinton presents the Medal of Freedom, America's highest civilian honor, to Cesar Chavez posthumously. Helen Chavez receives the medal at a White House ceremony

Fred Ross marches with Chavez during the Renewed Boycott Campaign of 1988.

Permissions

Ilan Stavans teaches at Amherst College.
He is Lewis-Sebring Professor in Latin American and Latino Culture
and Five College Fortieth Anniversary Professor.

Photograph: Sam Masinter